Made possible by a grant from
Fremont Area Community
Foundation

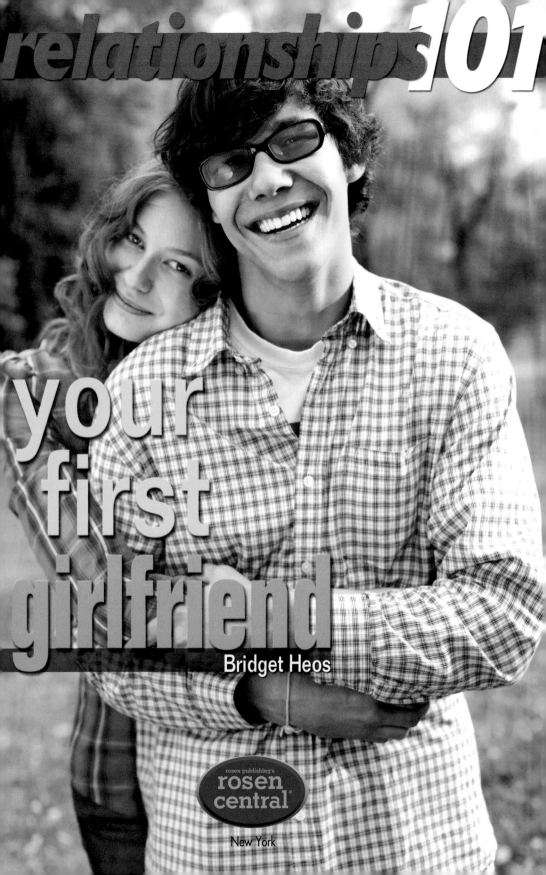

relationships 101

your first girlfriend

Bridget Heos

rosen publishing's
**rosen
central**

New York

Published in 2013 by The Rosen Publishing Group, Inc.
29 East 21st Street, New York, NY 10010

First Edition

Library of Congress Cataloging-in-Publication Data

Heos, Bridget.
Your first girlfriend/Bridget Heos.
     p. cm.—(Relationships 101)
Includes bibliographical references and index.
ISBN 978-1-4488-6830-8 (library binding)—ISBN 978-1-4488-6836-0 (pbk.)—ISBN 978-1-4488-6840-7 (6-pack)
1. Man-woman relationships—Juvenile literature. 2. Dating (Social customs)—Juvenile literature. 3. Couples—Juvenile literature. I. Title.
HQ801.H4724 2012
306.7—dc23

                                                                        2011048592

Manufactured in the United States of America

CPSIA Compliance Information: Batch #S12YA: For further information, contact Rosen Publishing, New York, New York, at 1-800-237-9932.

CONTENTS

12

33

Introduction

Getting to know your first girlfriend is a special time. But you probably have questions, too. In this book, we'll address questions that may arise in the course of your relationship.

You've been classmates for a while. She always seemed like a nice girl. Now, you're noticing other things about her, too. Like how her hair shines when the sun comes through the window. How she kicks the soccer ball right in the corner of the goal. How she laughs at things that you think are funny, too. You're starting to like this girl. But does she like you? How do you find out? What if she doesn't? What if she does? This book will guide you through having your first girlfriend, with all its ups and downs.

It includes information on how to strike up a conversation with a girl, how to tell if she likes you, and how to start a relationship. It gives ideas about fun things to do as a couple. It offers information on what good relationships and bad relationships look like. It offers insight into sexual activity and how middle schoolers really feel about it. It presents common problems that couples face and offers possible solutions.

Some problems are unsolvable, and the relationship ends. Here, you'll learn how to break up with a girl the right way. You'll also learn how to survive a breakup when it's her call. You'll learn how to take the high road even during a bad breakup. And you'll learn how to move on.

If you don't have a girlfriend yet, but would like one, there's information for you, too. You'll learn about being the kind of guy girls want to date. You'll also learn how to change your luck in love, whether you're saddled with a crush or like a nice girl who likes a mean guy. Hopefully, this advice will get you a little closer to having a first girlfriend. In the meantime, it will help you build confidence and be the best guy you can be. So let's get started.

CHAPTER ONE

YOU LIKE HER. NOW WHAT?

When you like somebody, the first step is to get to know her. You may already sort of know the girl. You know that you like her. Perhaps you've gone to school together or lived in the same neighborhood for several years. Even so, you may not really know her.

To get to know a girl, a phone call or text might seem easiest. But it's best to talk in person. Try to talk to her in the hall between classes. If you're nervous, ask your friends to join you. Together, you can talk to her and her friends. For instance, you could try to sit at the same lunch table. Or organize a group activity, such as a day at the park, a bowling night, or a movie night at somebody's house.

When you first talk to her, you may feel nervous. She won't mind that. Remember,

How can you tell if a girl likes you? Does this girl like this boy? It appears that she does. There are other ways to tell, too.

she may be nervous, too. Take a deep breath, stand tall, and try to have fun. To put her at ease, pay a compliment or make a friendly joke. Then, strike up a conversation. This may come easily to you. If not, keep in mind that the start of a conversation is the hardest.

To get the ball rolling, have a few conversation starters in mind. If one doesn't work, move onto the next. A good conversation starter might be something unusual that happened at school. For example, if there was a fire drill at school that day, you could talk about that. If nothing unusual happened, talk about something normal that you both experienced. Or there's the old standby: ask her how her day is going. You can talk about people you both know, but don't say anything negative about people. The same goes for complaining. Remember, you're trying to put your best foot forward.

If you don't know much about the girl, you can discreetly ask one of her friends what her interests are. This will make it easier to ask her questions about herself. For example, if her friends tell you she's an actress, you can ask her what plays she's been in. The main thing to know is that great conversationalists are actually great listeners.

Open-ended questions are best for getting conversations started. Asking, "Do you like having three brothers?" triggers a yes or no response. An open-ended way of asking the same question is, "What's it like being the only girl in your family?" This allows her to answer in a more thoughtful way. When asking questions, be interested in her life without prying. A prying question might be, "Do you dislike any of your brothers?" This sounds nosy and unkind to her family.

As important as questions are, you don't want the

conversation to be a series of them. She'll feel like she is being interrogated. Add your own thoughts and experiences. Be yourself and be honest, but don't overshare. Confiding something like, "…and that's when I developed my crippling fear of clowns," is an example of oversharing. At some point, your girlfriend will want to know all about you, but sharing too much too early can seem needy. Most girls want to get to know boys at a slower pace.

Once you've had a few casual conversations, you can take the next step. Give her a call or text her. If you feel uncomfortable, you can call to ask her about an assignment, and then talk for a little while afterward.

Texts, tweets, Facebook posts, or other social media may be part of your conversations. On the plus side, conversing in writing allows you to think about what to say. On the other hand, those words

Asking open-ended questions, being a good listener, and sharing — but not oversharing — are ways to keep a conversation going when you call a girl you like.

are out there for the world to see. Principals, teachers, parents, and other kids may read what you say. Even private messages and texts can be easily shared. An old saying goes, "Never say anything that you wouldn't want posted on a billboard." The saying certainly holds true for anything you put in writing.

Keep your texts, tweets, and posts positive and friendly. Feel free to joke, but make sure it doesn't come across wrong. In writing, you can't show your tone of voice. So, a joke can seem serious or mean-spirited. Also watch what others post. If people are posting about your newfound crush online, it can be uncomfortable. You can ignore them or ask them to stop. If you choose the latter, talk to them in person or over the phone. It's best not to be confrontational in tweets, texts, or Facebook posts. If things ever get out of hand online, talk to a trusted adult. Many schools have policies about online behavior.

Now that you've gotten to know each other, you're probably starting to sense whether or not she likes you as a potential boyfriend.

Does She Like You?

Relationships are a two-way street. Your next step is to find out if the girl you like likes you. Every girl is different. But here are some good signs:

- Her friends ask what you think of her.
- She steals glances at you. (Or, if she's shy, averts eye contact.)
- She laughs at your jokes.
- She flirts with you.
- She tries to run into you by showing up at places you will be.
- Her demeanor changes around you. (She becomes more nervous or more friendly.)

TALK ABOUT IT

There's a song about throwing a party for the broken-hearted. The lyrics say that it's a private party, open to members only. The joke is that, in truth, everybody is a member of the broken-hearted club. (Yes, it will even happen to the girl you like.) Ask a teenager or grown-up family member to tell you about one of his or her middle school heartbreaks. Notice how the person looks back on that moment now. It's unlikely that he or she is still upset about it.

- You converse easily.
- She frequently comments on your Facebook or Twitter posts.
- She texts or calls for various reasons (a question about homework, school, etc.).

Keep in mind her unique personality. A shy girl may act shy around everyone; a friendly girl might say hi to everybody. Be careful to discern a hunch that she likes you from wishful thinking. If you're not sure, ask a trusted friend. Sometimes, other people can tell when a couple likes each other before the couple knows it themselves.

If you think she likes you, ask her out. Again, this is best done in person. Kids at different schools have different ways of saying this. You might ask her to go out with you. This doesn't necessarily mean you'll go anywhere. Rather, it means that you're now girlfriend and

After spending time talking and hanging out after school or with other friends, you might take it to the next step: becoming boyfriend and girlfriend.

boyfriend. Or you may simply tell her that you like her.

If she says yes, or that she likes you, too, and agrees to be your girlfriend, congratulations! We talk about that in chapter 3. If she says no…ouch. That hurts. It's OK to feel sad, disappointed, and embarrassed. You might even feel the physical effects of heartbreak: an upset stomach, a hollow feeling inside, a headache. Let yourself feel sad for a while. It's OK to cry and talk about it with people close to you whom you trust. But eventually you will need to pick yourself up and brush yourself off.

Here's the main thing: if you ask a girl out and she says no, that is the end of the story. Don't ask again. Don't let on that you still like her. Don't act mad. Try not to act too embarrassed. If possible, have a sense of humor about it. Most of all, don't give up on yourself. It's not the end of your story! It only makes you available for a girl who thinks you're the coolest guy ever. She's out there.

Sometimes, you accept the heartbreak and move on. Other times, you continue liking the person. That's called a crush, and it feels just like it sounds. In fact, it's so painful (and so common) that it gets its own chapter.

CRUSHES, AWKWARDNESS, AND OTHER UNLUCKY THINGS

Y ou can't help that you have a crush. And you can't stop it from, well, crushing you. But you can decide how to respond. That way, when you look back on your crush later, you'll at least be proud of how you handled it.

If a girl doesn't like you, be discreet about the crush. Don't pursue her. You can talk to a friend about your feelings, but don't tell the whole world. Feel free to write down your thoughts, but don't post them on Facebook. It will make her uncomfortable, and you'll likely end up feeling embarrassed. Whatever you do, do not be mean or cruel to her. Believe it or not, you'll eventually like somebody else. In order to have a chance with her, you'll need to have your act together.

Here's how to handle a crush: don't try to stop thinking about her. Often, when you tell yourself not to think about

If you have a crush on someone, it may be hard to take your mind off her. Rather than trying to do so, find other things to occupy your mind.

something, that's exactly what you think about. Example: Don't think about Halloween candy. Don't think about your favorite kind. Also, don't think about your least favorite kind. What are you thinking about? Instead, focus on what you can do in addition to your crush. In other words, think of your crush as a hobby, not a full-time job.

To take your mind off your crush, learn how to do something new, such as play the guitar, play chess, or do a card trick. Or practice harder at something. Become the guy who pitches a killer Wiffle ball or has an incredible free-throw percentage. You can always go for pure entertainment, too. Read that book series you've heard about. Plan a movie marathon with your friends. Anything that draws your concentration away from your crush is time well spent.

Now is also a good time to focus on the people who love you. Spend more time with your friends (and don't talk about your crush the whole time!). Spend time with family. Offer to help with a project around the house. Take lunch once a week to a grandparent. Someday, your crush will be a distant memory. But the time you spent getting to know more about a grandparent won't be.

You can also get to know other people better. Strike up a conversation with people in your class. Ask them about themselves. This takes your mind off your own distress. And you might make a new friend, too. If you go on Facebook, make a point of checking other people's status updates, not just your crush's. Don't comment on your crush's Facebook or Twitter posts. It will give the impression that you still like her, which is exactly the impression you're trying not to make. Your comments may also be misunderstood. If you comment excessively, your crush may

Spending time with friends and pursuing new endeavors, whether a sport, hobby, or job, can help take your mind off a crush or other relationship problem.

see your actions as stalking or harassment. That type of behavior is unacceptable, so be careful to avoid it.

Other ideas: spend time outside. It's amazing how much better sunlight can make you feel. Get a part-time job or join a youth group. This will introduce you to people out-side of school—a great way to take your mind off a class-mate crush. Most importantly, know that at some point, your crush on this person will go away. You'll like somebody new. And that somebody will like you, too.

Other Unlucky-in- Love Things

In addition to crushes, there are several speed bumps on the road to true love. Here are a few.

She's Out of Your League

Some grown-ups will tell you it's nonsense to think this way. You're a perfectly nice boy!

Any girl would be lucky to have you! That is likely true. But like it or not, there are "leagues" in middle school. An older, more mature, or extremely popular girl, for instance, may be out of your league. Rest assured that at some point, there are no leagues, just people. But for now, if you think a girl is out of your league, tread lightly. Ask a friend what he thinks. Be friendly to her, but in a way that shows you're happy to be friends only. If she truly seems to like you, go for it. If you're not sure, it's best to play the waiting game. Focus on being a happy person and a good guy. Pursue your interests and go after your goals. Five or ten years from now, the girl who was out of your league will think you're a catch.

She's in Love with a Mean Guy

This one can be hard to understand. What does a nice girl see in a guy who is clearly her opposite? Everyone is attracted to confidence. If you see a girl with a mean guy, she's likely attracted to his confidence, not his jerkiness. If you're both confident and a nice guy, you will eventually get the girl. You've probably seen this play out among popular kids in your class. A confident—but inconsiderate— kid runs the show early on. But as time passes, saying mean things, excluding kids, and pushing people around becomes uncool. If that kid doesn't change, he loses friends. The same is true of confident but jerky guys.

You'd Like a Girlfriend, but Most Girls Don't Know You Exist

This is actually one of the luckiest of the unlucky things. Your mind isn't set on one girl. Instead, you can focus on being "the Guy a Girl Wants to Date." What kind of guy is

How do you get a girl to like you? You don't need to be the most handsome or coolest kid. Instead, focus on being a good guy and being true to yourself.

that? In a study conducted by *For Young Men Only*, 91 percent of girls said they'd prefer an average-looking, nice, and funny guy to a gorgeous, athletic guy who has a reputation of being full of himself. Top traits girls admire are a sense of humor, thoughtfulness, and self-confidence. Last on their list of desirable traits are buff body, athletic, rich, and cocky.

So who is this average-looking nice and funny guy? You! If you've liked a girl who didn't like you back, that doesn't mean you're missing some magical "It" factor. It means she wasn't the right girl for you. Make sure you're being a good guy, and a girl will like you soon enough. Girls notice how guys treat classmates, teachers, and family. They know that you would likely treat them the same way. With that in mind:

- Be a guy who says nice things to people. Girls like boys who are kind, which can include saying nice things to them that they genuinely mean.

- Be a guy who doesn't follow the crowd. Girls like boys who think for themselves.
- Be a guy who can laugh at himself. Girls like guys with a sense of humor. At the same time, don't be super silly. That makes you look foolish instead of funny.
- Be a guy who knows how to act online. Girls like guys with good social skills. Online, evidence of good or bad social skills stays around for a long time.
- Be a confident guy. Stand up straight. Look people in the eye. Do the right thing, and don't worry what people think. Girls like boys who are confident.
- Be a polite guy. Open doors for others, help carry things, share your snacks, and give up your seat to someone who

HELP! WHEN I'M NERVOUS, IT SHOWS!

Nature plays a trick on some of us. When we're nervous, we sweat, feel nauseated, or tremble. If it's an extreme condition, talk to your parents. Together, you can discuss your anxiety with your doctor. If it's more minor, here are a couple of things to try. First, practice overcoming your nerves in low-stakes situations. Try talking to a nice girl who you don't have a crush on. If you're visibly shaken, tell her that talking to new people makes you nervous, but it's something you're working on. Second, take baby steps toward your goal. Don't try striking up a conversation right away with the girl you like. Just smile and nod when you walk by. Next time you see her, say hi. Little by little, you'll feel more comfortable around her.

needs it. Girls like boys who are thoughtful.

- Be a nice guy. Being nice isn't the opposite of being mean. Being nice means going out of your way to help out someone else. Is there a kid in your class who doesn't fit in? A nice guy doesn't make fun of him. But a nice guy also sticks up for him.

Incidentally, all these things help you lead a good life—whether you get the girl right away or not. It's great to be a good guy, but you're probably also wondering how important looks are. Girls don't put as much emphasis on handsomeness as you might think. But they do like a guy to look his best. Get exercise, and shower every day. Wear deodorant. You don't have to wear expensive clothes, but wear a clean shirt, and don't look grubby. (Choose jeans over sweatpants, for instance.) Remember, girls are attracted to confidence. Get a haircut that you like, whether it follows a trend or not. Wear clothes that reflect your personal style. These things will make you feel confident.

YOU'RE A COUPLE. NOW WHAT?

Having a girlfriend is like having a new friend… who you like as more than a friend. Your parents will probably think you're too young to go on dates as a couple. Here are some fun things you can do as a group:

- Watch a movie at a friend's house.
- Go to a school event, such as the carnival or a mixer or dance.
- Go to each other's activities, such as a game or play. (If she's in a play or recital, it's customary to bring her flowers.)
- Go to a ball game.
- Go bowling.
- Go swimming in the summer or sledding in the winter.
- Go on a bike ride, play football at the park, or play a game you liked as kids, like hide-and-seek.
- Have a video game tournament.
- Do something nice, like

Bowling is one activity you and your girlfriend can do together. If you're still getting to know each other, it's easy to invite some other friends as well. It gives you time to talk but also keeps things active.

raking your grandparents' yard or taking a younger sibling to the park.

It's fun to have a girlfriend. But it's also important to have a good relationship. In a good relationship, you have fun together. You have common interests or points of view. You attend things that are important to her, and she does the same for you. At the same time, you accept each other's differences. You do your own things sometimes.

In a good relationship, conversation comes easily. Time passes quickly when you talk. You feel like you can talk about anything, whether serious or light-hearted. You respect each other's beliefs. You may not always agree, but you argue civilly. You try to get along and don't bicker just to bicker.

In a good relationship, you show in ways big and small that you care. You help each other. You share things. You stand up for each other. You inspire each other to be your best and express concerns. For instance, if she's studying for a big test, you give her time to do that. You may offer to bring frozen yogurt for a study break, too. If, on the other hand, she's putting off a big assignment, you might encourage her to get started. Keep in mind that little things can mean a lot in a relationship. Does she like having her hand held? Does she like making plans together? Does she like help with projects? Does she like little gifts? Try to find out what "little things" matter most to your girlfriend.

As you get to know your girlfriend, you'll get to know her friends and family, too. Be friendly to her family and especially kind to younger siblings. If you're invited to a family activity, attend if it's OK with your parents. As she introduces you to family members, try to remember their names so that you can talk to

When spending time around your girlfriend's family, be sure to be nice to her siblings and polite to her parents. Maybe you can help a younger sibling with his homework.

them later. If you're not sure what to do at a family party, offer to help with something.

The same is true of getting to know her friends. Learn their names, say hi when you see them, and be able to carry on a conversation. If you don't like one of her friends, keep that to yourself, unless the friend is mean to you or bad for your girlfriend (she takes dangerous risks, for instance). In that case, you can state your concerns. But it's up to your girlfriend to decide what to do. Also, if your girlfriend argues with her friends, stay out of it. They'll reconcile eventually, and it will be awkward if you got in the middle.

At the same time, keep your own friends. Maintain strong ties with your family. Continue to pursue your personal interests. No matter how good a relationship is, never let your whole life revolve around one person.

Physical Relationships

You may have your first girlfriend before either of you feels old enough to hold hands. And that's fine. Other times, the two of you may be ready for your first kiss. That's OK, too. But beyond the first kiss, things can get tricky.

For one thing, a girl wants a guy who has her back. Girls tend to want a physical relationship later than boys do. If she feels pressured to move too fast, she'll think you don't have her best interests at heart. She might go along with the physical relationship to be close to you. But it puts her in a bad spot. Talk to her before pursuing a physical relationship, and always ask for her permission before becoming physical with her in any way. You owe it to her to find out how she really feels, as well as what she is OK and not OK with doing physically.

It's important to discuss boundaries — and stick to them — in a physical relationship so that neither of you gets hurt or gets in over your head.

Finally, one extremely important note: no means no. If your girlfriend wants to stop, you must stop. Pushing a girl past the point where she says no is unacceptable. It's disrespectful and dangerous and, in many cases, against the law. Listen to your girlfriend and respect her boundaries at all times.

If you both want a physical relationship, how do you know you're ready? The two of you should feel comfortable enough to talk about it. Find out the "steps" of a physical relationship, sometimes described as "bases." Decide how far the two of you are comfortable going. Stick to that comfort zone.

Until your late teens, at the earliest, it's unlikely that you can handle the physical and emotional risks that a sexual relationship brings. Contrary to what you may see on TV or in the movies, sex is not carefree. Sex can lead to sexually

HELP! PEOPLE ARE SAYING I'M GAY. I DON'T KNOW IF I AM OR NOT.

Let's look at this as two separate issues. First, you're wondering if you're gay. Give yourself time to learn the answer. Be true to yourself. Yes, you may be gay. Or you may not be. It's not up to other people to rush this self-discovery.

Second, people are saying things about you. If they're your friends, they might have good intentions. At the same time, it's up to you to explore your own sexuality. If you are gay, it's also up to you to decide when and who to tell. Let your friends know your position on this. But also recognize that their questions are an invitation to open up if you choose.

If people are saying this in a mean way, they're being bullies. Keep your cool, but stand up for yourself. Realize that the bully speaks only for himself or herself. Don't assume that other people feel the same way. Tell your friends and family what's going on. It's important to have allies.

Finally, stay safe and know your rights. Many schools have anti-bullying policies. Document instances of bullying. That way, if the situation escalates, school officials will see a pattern. Keep your personal safety in mind. Let your family and school authorities know of potentially dangerous situations (a threat of being beat up, for instance). Until the situation is resolved, travel in numbers.

transmitted diseases (STDs) or pregnancy. Even if it doesn't (and without contraception, it will; with contraception, it could), it will make your relationship and your life less carefree.

Biologically, sex is for reproduction. Many feelings surrounding sex have to do with providing a home for a healthy baby, whether or not sex actually results in pregnancy. This is why men and women, after sex, can feel the need to be closer emotionally and physically. At a young age, you may feel uncomfortable with this level of closeness and seriousness. It's like you have the worries of a married couple… but you're in middle school. Not a good feeling. And you don't have to have sex to feel this way. Being sexually involved in other ways can bring about the same feelings.

If you and your girlfriend decide to have sex, contraception must be discussed and obtained, sometimes months in advance. Because a teen pregnancy can be devastating, it's a good idea to use two forms of birth control.

You may not be ready for a physical relationship. But you can start thinking about when you'll be ready. These beliefs will be influenced by your family, community, religion, and personal experiences. You may decide that you'll be ready after marriage, when you have a serious girlfriend later in life, or when you're older and ready to take on more responsibility. Forming these beliefs and sticking to them is a mature thing to do.

If you do feel like your relationship is getting physical, talk to your parents or a trusted adult. The only fool-proof contraception is abstinence.

HELP! MY FRIEND IS IN A HURTFUL RELATIONSHIP.

Forms of abuse include physical, sexual, and emotional abuse. How can you help a friend or girlfriend who is being abused?

- *If you believe abuse is happening, ask.*
- *Listen to him or her.*
- *Let him or her know that you believe what you're hearing.*
- *Express your concern for his or her safety. Name a few instances that are of particular concern. If others, such as a sibling, are also in danger, point that out.*
- *Give him or her resources. Offer to accompany your friend as he or she calls an abuse hotline or talks to a counselor.*
- *Tell a trusted adult. Tell your friend that you are going to do this so that you don't destroy the trust between you. Explain that you are concerned for his or her safety.*

But contraception is much more effective than nothing at all at preventing pregnancy and STDs. Especially at such a young age, when a pregnancy can be devastating, it's best to use two forms of contraception, such as a condom and birth control pills. Birth control pills need to be prescribed months before having sex. If you or your girlfriend aren't ready to plan for this, you're definitely not ready to have sex. And that's normal. A big misconception about sex among teens is that "everybody is doing it." That's not true. See the end of the book for myths and facts on this.

Only a small percentage of middle schoolers have sex, and even older teens place many priorities above a sexual relationship. In reality, everybody isn't doing it, and it's normal to want to wait.

HANDLING CONFLICTS AND BREAKING UP

Every relationship has problems. Those involving trust, respect, and a need for control are deal breakers. If there is a pattern of you or your girlfriend doing any of the following, call it quits right away:

- Playing games (liking someone one day and not the next)
- Not showing up for a planned activity
- Dating other people secretly
- Repeating things told in confidence
- Saying mean things to you, privately or in public
- Any physical roughness or violence
- Constantly calling or texting
- Extreme jealousy
- Not wanting the other to see family or friends

Other problems are normal and can often be resolved. These involve time and communication. You have to spend

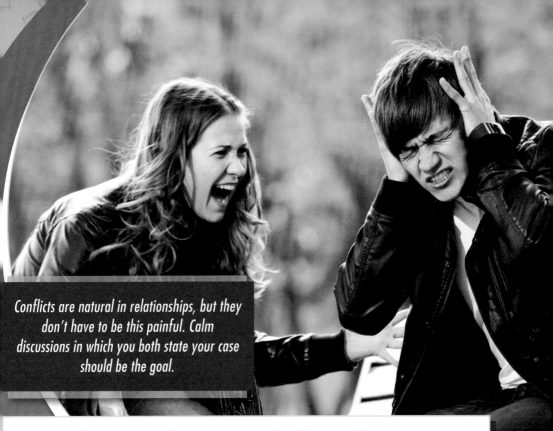

Conflicts are natural in relationships, but they don't have to be this painful. Calm discussions in which you both state your case should be the goal.

time together to get to know each other. If you go to separate schools, you may not see each other. This can cause you to drift apart. One of you may want to spend more time together, or you may disagree on how to spend time together. She may like to go places, whereas you prefer to play video games at home. Both situations call for compromise. Finally, you may bicker when you're together. If you're often annoyed with each other, you should spend less time together. If it continues, it's time to call it quits.

A final problem area—and perhaps the biggest—is communication. Instead of being direct, people often play guessing games. Let's say that your girlfriend is five minutes late to meet you in the library. No big deal. The next day, she's fifteen minutes late. Kind of annoying, but you don't say anything. The next day, she's thirty minutes late. When she arrives, you're mad at her. But you refuse to tell her why. She should be able to figure it out on her own.

The "Guess why I'm mad at you" approach rarely works. Of course, your girlfriend knows that you're mad at her for being late. But she doesn't understand why it's a big deal. Why didn't you study without her? That's what she would have done. The problem is, what's frustrating to one person can be no big deal to another. It's best to explain, in a calm way, why you're frustrated. You could say, "When you're this late, it makes me think you're a no-show. And it also makes me think that you don't care that I think that." She will realize that lateness means different things to you.

If the tables are turned, and she is mad at you for an unknown reason, open the conversation. Tell her that you see she's mad and ask if she wants to talk about it. Listen to her without being defensive. Let her know that you understand what she's saying. Apologize if you did something wrong. If not, tell her that you see things differently. Try to reach a compromise. If neither of you is willing to bend, then it's time to call it quits.

Communication also involves opening up to each other. Nobody's life is perfect, and as your relationship progresses, you'll discuss serious things. It's important to know that boys and girls are raised to discuss problems differently. Say your girlfriend calls to tell you her father lost his job. While she describes what things are like at home, you wonder how her dad can get a new job. When she pauses, you ask if he's had any interviews. She says that he has some lined up. As far as you're concerned, that ends the conversation. Granted, he doesn't have a job yet, but there's nothing more anyone can do, so why talk about it?

You may have a lot on your plate, including school, sports, work, and family concerns. If you need space, you can let your girlfriend know. Or she may be able to help you through it.

You ask your girlfriend if she's finished her math homework. Then, you hear crying on the other line. What went wrong? When discussing a problem, boys often want to jump to the solution. You're trying to be helpful. But girls like to discuss the problem itself. It's important to hear her out. On the flip side, when you have a problem, your girlfriend may want you to talk about it at length. But it's OK to discuss problems in your own way.

Sometimes, when you're dealing with your own problems, you feel like you don't have time for a relationship. By the time you deal with family, schoolwork, and sports or clubs, you have nothing left. If you feel this way, let your girlfriend know. At the same time, don't sell her short. She may be able to help you get through this.

Breaking Up

At the end of a relationship, you face the challenge of breaking up. The first rule of breaking up is…to actually break up. It may seem less

HELP! I NEED TO TALK TO SOMEBODY ABOUT GIRL TROUBLE.

It's OK to talk to a friend about relationship problems. If you have a friend who is a girl, she might have unique insight into your girlfriend's point of view. Talk to a friend who will be discreet. And don't say things that will embarrass your girlfriend. In particular, don't share things that she has confided in you.

painful to let her "figure it out" by drifting away. Really, that leaves her in the lurch. Instead, tell her how you feel in the nicest way possible. Always break up in person, never by e-mail, phone, or text. Be honest. Don't lead her to believe the breakup is temporary. At the same time, brutal honesty isn't called for. If there's a clear reason for the breakup, such as a breach of trust, you can tell her. Otherwise, simply say you're not right for each other, which is probably true.

After the breakup, treat her with respect. Don't avoid her. Say hello when you see her. If, by chance, she keeps pursuing you, be frank. Let her know that you're not going to get back together. If she is acting out her anger toward you, talk to her about it. She may be hurt, but as long as you broke up in a nice way, she shouldn't be mean to you.

If your girlfriend breaks up with you, many of the same rules apply. Listen to what she says. Ask questions if you have

After a breakup, you may feel sad or angry. You may feel blindsided. Remember that you'll get through this. Act in a manner that won't embarrass you later.

any, but don't try to convince her to change her mind. Afterward, you may feel a sense of relief. Or you might feel blindsided.

In that case, it's OK to be sad, but try not to show it in front of her, at least not for long.

Be nice to her and say hello when you see her, but don't stick around to chitchat. It's best to keep your distance, at least at first. Try not to brood about the breakup. If you wish you'd done things differently, learn from your mistakes and move on. If you did your best, don't second-guess yourself. And don't take the breakup personally. You weren't right for each other. If you think back, you probably noticed this, too (or will eventually). Know that most people don't find true love their first try. Most people simply aren't meant to spend their whole lives together. That's why true love is so precious.

The main idea, when someone breaks up with you, is to take the high road. Even if she breaks up with you in an insensitive manner, be civil. When two people fight

HELP! I CAN'T SEEM TO GET OVER THIS BREAKUP!

A breakup can be a stressful event. It's normal to feel sad. If the sadness continues for too long or gets worse, talk to a parent or trusted adult. Sometimes, stress can trigger depression, a treatable illness that requires medical attention.

publicly, nobody asks who started it. Instead, both people end up looking bad. In particular, avoid online confrontations or mean text messages. If she's doing these things to you, ask her to stop, and if she doesn't, talk to a trusted grown-up. Quit social media for a while if necessary.

Some breakups are harder to take than others. If you are crushed by the breakup:

- Avoid seeing her.
- Focus on doing things you like.
- Spend time with friends and family.
- Take care of yourself.
- Pick yourself up. Remember that you were OK without her and will be OK again.
- Be a guy she would want to date (or more likely, somebody else would like to date).

You can't avoid your ex-girlfriend forever, especially if you go to the same school. As time passes, you'll see her without feeling awkward. And you'll understand that the breakup wasn't the end of the world. There's no rush to find a new girlfriend. This is the time to enjoy your friends and family.

Whether you're still with your first girlfriend or not, be proud of yourself. You took a chance and pursued a girl you liked. That takes courage. Whether the relationship lasts for a week, a year, or forever, you'll be a better and wiser person for having experienced it.

MYTHS AND FACTS

Myth: Most teens and preteens don't feel that they need to be in love to have sex.
Fact: In reality, most girls and 50 percent of boys want to be in love before having sex, according to Sex Ed: Growing Up, Relationships, and Sex.

Myth: Most kids in their early teens are having sex.
Fact: According to Growing Up Too Fast: The Rimm Report on the Secret World of America's Middle Schoolers, *only a small percentage of middle schoolers are sexually active.*

Myth: Teens are preoccupied with sex.
Fact: It's actually at the bottom of their priorities. Here are priorities, in order, for teenage girls, according to Sex Ed: Growing Up, Relationships, and Sex: *close friendships with other girls, doing well at school, friendships with boys, having a boyfriend, sports, having a sexual relationship with a boy.* For boys, the priorities are: *doing well in school, friendships with other boys, friendships with girls, sports, having a girlfriend, having a sexual relationship with a girl.*

10 GREAT QUESTIONS TO ASK A GUIDANCE COUNSELOR

1. How do I get girls to notice me?

2. How can I tell if a girl likes me?

3. How can I show a girl that I like her?

4. What should my girlfriend and I do if we want to have a more physical relationship?

5. How do I break up with a girl?

6. How do I handle a breakup?

7. How can I help a friend in a bad relationship?

8. How can I help a friend who is being abused?

9. What do I do if something embarrassing is posted about me online?

10. What if I don't know if I'm gay or straight?

GLOSSARY

abuse Hurtful treatment, whether physical, emotional, or sexual.

anxiety A state of excessive worry or nervousness in which symptoms may be physical, such as trembling or sweating.

birth control Contraception. In some cases, such as birth control pills, it prevents pregnancy but not sexually transmitted diseases.

communication The act of sharing thoughts, feelings, and information by talking, body language, or writing.

contraception Any measure that prevents pregnancy.

conversationalist One who enjoys and is good at talking with others.

crush An infatuation, or a person with whom someone is infatuated.

dating The act of meeting socially with a girlfriend or boyfriend.

depression A medical condition in which a person feels hopeless and inadequate.

discreet Careful about what is said.

gay Homosexual; having sexual desire for those of the same sex.

sexually active Having sex or engaging in other sexual acts with someone.

sexually transmitted disease (STD) A disease that can be passed from one person to another through sexual intercourse.

social media Web sites in which users share information, thoughts, or feelings.

stress Mental or physical pressure felt because of an external situation.

trust The belief in someone's dependability to do the right thing.

FOR MORE INFORMATION

Advocates for Youth
2000 M Street NW, Suite 750
Washington, DC 20036
(202) 419-3420
Web site: http://www.advocatesforyouth.org
Advocates for Youth helps young people make responsible decisions
    about their health and sexuality.

American Medical Association
515 N. State Street
Chicago, IL 60654
(800) 621-8335
Web site: http://www.ama-assn.org
The American Medical Association provides information on a variety
    of matters, including adolescent health.

BBYO
2020 K Street NW, 7th Floor
Washington, DC 20006
(202) 857-6633
Web site: http://bbyo.org
BBYO connects and inspires teens to lead Jewish lives while making
    a difference in the world.

Canadian Association for Adolescent Health (CAAH)
Section médecine de l'adolescence
Sainte-Justine Hospital
7th floor, 2nd bloc
3175 Côte Sainte-Catherine
Montreal QC H3T 1C5

(514) 345-9959
Web site: http://www.acsa-caah.ca/en/Home.aspx
The Canadian Association for Adolescent Health promotes health in
    adolescents.

Gay Straight Alliance Network
1550 Bryant Street, Suite 800
San Francisco, CA 94103
(415) 552-4229
Web site: http://www.gsanetwork.org
The Gay Straight Alliance Network empowers students to fight
    homophobia in schools.

Web Sites

Due to the changing nature of Internet links, Rosen Publishing has
developed an online list of Web sites related to the subject of this
book. This site is updated regularly. Please use this link to access
the list:

http://www.rosenlinks.com/r101/gf

FOR FURTHER READING

Bell, Ruth. *Changing Bodies, Changing Lives: Expanded Third Edition: A Book for Teens on Sex and Relationships.* New York, NY: Random House, 2011.

Berman, Steve. *Speaking Out: LGBTQ Youth Stand Up.* Valley Falls, NY: Bold Strokes Books, 2011.

Boyett, Jason. *A Guy's Guide to Life: How to Become a Man in 224 Pages or Less.* Nashville, TN: Thomas Nelson, 2010.

Covey, Sean. *The 6 Most Important Decisions You'll Ever Make: A Guide for Teens.* Clearwater, FL: Touchstone, 2006.

Fox, Annie. *The Teen Survival Guide to Dating & Relating: Real-World Advice for Teens on Guys, Girls, Growing Up, and Getting Along.* Minneapolis, MN: Free Spirit, 2005.

Harris, Robie, and Michael Emberley. *It's Perfectly Normal: Changing Bodies, Growing Up, Sex, and Sexual Health.* Somerville, MA: Candlewick, 2009.

Kaplan, Arie. *Dating and Relationships: Navigating the Social Scene (A Young Man's Guide to Contemporary Issues).* New York, NY: Rosen Publishing Group, 2012.

Madaras, Lynda, and Area Madaras. *My Body, My Self for Boys (What's Happening to My Body?).* New York, NY: New Market Press, 2007.

Markovics, Joyce. *Relationship Smarts: How to Navigate Dating, Friendships, Family Relationships, and More (USA Today Teen Wise Guides: Time, Money, and Relationships).* Minneapolis, MN: Lerner, 2012.

Pfeifer, Kate Gruenwald. *American Medical Association Boy's Guide to Becoming a Teen.* San Francisco, CA: Jossey-Bass, 2006.

Toussaint, Jonathon. *How to Talk to Girls.* Sydney, Australia: Allen and Unwin, 2011.

Bell, Ruth. *Changing Bodies, Changing Lives: A Book for Teens on Sex and Relationships.* New York, NY: Times Books, 2011.

Bridges, John. *50 Things Every Young Gentleman Should Know: What to Do, When to Do It, and Why.* Nashville, TN: Rutledge Hill, 2006.

Chapman, Gary. *The Five Love Languages of Teenagers.* Chicago, IL: Northfield, 2010.

Elias, Maurice, Steven Tobias, and Brian Friedlander. *Raising Emotionally Intelligent Teenagers.*New York, NY: Harmony, 2002.

Feldhahn, Jeff, and Eric Rice. *For Young Men Only.* Colorado Springs, CO: Multnomah Books, 2008.

Fox, Annie. Elizabeth Verdick, ed. *Can You Relate?* Minneapolis, MN: Free Spirit, 1999.

Gaughan, Colleen. Interview with author. *Social Media and Teens.* September 21, 2011.

Goodstein, Anastasia. *Totally Wired: What Teens and Tweens Are Really Doing Online.* New York, NY: St. Martin's, 2007.

Hughes, Kevin. "Confessions of a Gutsy Gay Teen." DoSomething.org. Retrieved September. 3, 2011 (http://www.dosomething.org/tipsandtools/confessions-a-gutsy-gay-teen).

Jackson, Lindsay. *101 Things Teens Should Know.* Kansas City, MO: Andrews-McMeel, 2002.

Rimm, Sylvia. *Growing Up Too Fast: The Rimm Report on the Secret World of America's Middle Schoolers.* Emmaus, PA: Rodale, 2005.

Stoppard, Miriam. *Sex Ed: Growing Up, Relationships, and Sex.* New York, NY: DK, 1997.

INDEX

About the Author

Bridget Heos is the author of several young adult nonfiction titles on topics ranging from biographies to science to states. Prior to being an author for teens, she was a newspaper reporter and freelance journalist. She lives in Kansas City with her husband and three sons.

Photo Credits

Cover, p. 1 Sergey Furtaev/Shutterstock.com; pp. 3 (top), 12 Comstock/Thinkstock; pp. 3 (bottom), 33 © istockphoto.com/ Dmitry Kalinovsky; pp. 4–5 Doug Menuez/Photodisc/Thinkstock; pp. 6, 14, 22, 32 © istockphoto.com/Chris Schmidt; p. 7 Lite Productions/Thinkstock; pp. 9, 37 istockphoto/Thinkstock; p. 15 Hemera/Thinkstock; p. 17 © Jim West/The Image Works; p. 19 Eyecandy Images/Thinkstock; p. 23 David Stuart/Digital Vision/ Getty Images; p. 25 Eric Audras/Getty Images; p. 27 Goodshoot/Thinkstock; p. 29 Charles Thatcher/Stone/Getty Images; p. 35 Jupiterimages/Comstock/Thinkstock; multiple interior background (orange) istockphoto.com/stereohype.

Designer: Nelson Sa; Editor: Bethany Bryan;
Photo Researcher: Amy Feinberg